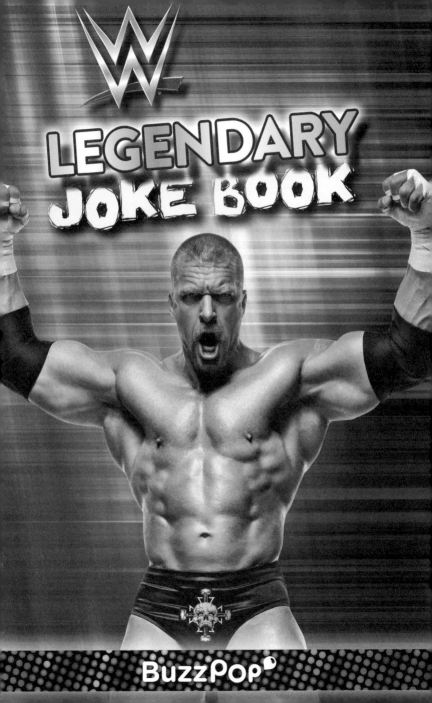

BuzzPop

An imprint of Little Bee Books

251 Park Avenue South, New York, NY 10010

HEY, YOU, YEAH, YOU!

Heard any good jokes lately? Good jokes are okay, but if you want great jokes—sidesplitting, gut-busting, knee-slapping, superjokes—you came to the right place! The rest of this book is filled with championship chuckles about your favorite WWE Superstars, Legends, events, and personalities. Every one of them is guaranteed to make you the Heavyweight of Hilarity! The Great One of Glee! Mr. or Ms. Funny in the Bank!

These jokes are so hilarious, you're guaranteed to have the first *and* the last laugh!

Why do WWE Superstars' fingers hurt?

Because their rings are square!

Why were Gene Okerlund's pants always so angry?

Because they were **MEAN JEANS**!

What's a WWE Superstar's favorite candy?

An **ARM BAR**!

4

Why do sailors make good WWE Superstars?

Because they already know the ropes!

What do you call Nia Jax when she has three eyes?

Niiia Jax.

Where does Beth Phoenix
shop online?

GLAMAZON Prime.

What do you get when you cross storm clouds with The Big Dog?

Roman **RAINS**.

What do you call the Heartbreak Kid when he stays up past his bedtime?

YAWN Michaels.

What did John Cena say when he ate at the Japanese restaurant?

You can't sashi-mi!

Which WWE Legend
don't you want at
your picnic?

Andre the Gi-ant.

What do you call two
WWE Superstars
arguing over chips?

A **SNACKDOWN**.

What's The Man's favorite bird?

A Becky Finch.

Why can't koalas be WWE Superstars?

They always get dis-koala-fied!

Who stole all the women's cheese?

Rowdy Ronda Mousey.

Which WWE Legend can't be trusted to watch your pet?

George "The Animal" Stealer.

What type of sandwich do AJ Styles, Luke Gallows, and Karl Anderson always eat for lunch?

The **CLUB**.

What was the pirate's favorite part of HBK and Triple H's treasure map?

D !

What did the referee count
when he went to the dentist?

One, **TOOTH**, three!

Who's that guy who's always
lying down in the ring?

You mean **MATT**?

What wakes The New
Day up every morning?

COFFEE Kingston!

What's the scariest treat you can get on Halloween?

Candy Kane.

What happens when K.O. takes out a loan?

Kevin's Owin'.

What do you call Kofi, Big E, and Xavier when they get sad?

The **BLUE** Day.

What do you call a group of mean chickens?

The Hen-W-O.

What did The IIconics say to the ship captain?

"Aye, aye!"

Which WWE Title is defended at the circus?

The Inter-clown-tinental Championship.

What is every WWE Champion's favorite part of a book?

The **TITLE**!

What happens when there are two WWE Superstars but only one bathroom?

A **BLADDER** Match.

Did you hear about the contest between the two rabbits?

It was a **HARE** vs. **HARE** Match!

How do NXT Superstars celebrate in England?

With NXTea parties.

What is The Money's favorite condiment?

McMayonnaise.

How did Seth Rollins propose to Becky Lynch?

He gave her a ring!

What happens when 30 Superstars all go for the same football?

A Royal Fumble.

What happens when The Phenomenal One has no cavities?

AJ Smiles.

What do you get when you cross Drake Maverick with Ricochet?

Drake Mave-Ricochet.

Who is a fish's favorite Superstar?

FIN Bálor.

What is The Master of the 619's favorite cereal?

Mysteri-Os!

Who gives the best valentines in WWE?

Jeff and Matt **HEART**-y!

What is The Wicked Witch of WWE's favorite food?

BLISS Cheese.

What lives in a swamp, but is never late for tea?

The British Bullfrog.

What does The Miz call his mother?

"The Ms."

Why did The Million Dollar Man put his money in the freezer?

He wanted cold hard cash!

Drew McIntyre Baron Corbin, and Samoa Joe are all on a sinking ship. Who would be saved?

The fans!

What do Elias and Dracula have in common?

They're both a pain in the neck!

How did Charlotte win the first Raw Women's Championship?

With **FLAIR**!

How does Ember Moon cut her hair?

Sh-eclipse it!

Knock, knock.

Who's there?

Boo.

Boo WHO?

Boo **BARON CORBIN** whenever you have a chance!

27

What's every tag team's favorite fruit?

A **PEAR**.

Which WWE Superstar is the best at basketball?

Dribble H.

What does Shane McMahon say every Easter?

"Here comes the bunny!"

RANDY SAVAGE

What do you call Macho Man stuck between two pieces of bread?

A Randy Sammich.

OOH YEAH!

What happened when Triple H's puppy graduated college?

He got a pet-degree.

Knock, knock.

Who's there?

Ali.

Ali who?

Al-eat all my vegetables if I can go to **WRESTLEMANIA**!

Why did the arena get so hot a few hours after *SmackDown Live* ended?

All the **FAN**S left.

Which WWE division doesn't get enough rest?

The **SNOOZERWEIGHTS**!

What weighs more, a ton of feathers, or a ton of Baron Corbin fans?

A ton of feathers—there's no such thing as a ton of Baron Corbin fans!

Where does Bray Wyatt hide his dinner rolls?

The Firefly **BUN** House.

Which planet is most like WWE?

Saturn—it has the most **RINGS**!

What do you call Randy Orton when he's doing dishes?

The Wiper.

Knock, knock.

Who's there?

Natalya.

Natalya who?

Nat-al-ya can go to **SUMMERSLAM** unless all ya finish your chores!

Which tag team can never get straight As?

The B-Team!

What was the geometry teacher's favorite submission hold?

The **ANGLE** Lock.

$$= a^{\frac{1}{n}} \quad (a+b)^2 = a^2 + 2ab$$

$$\sin^2 \alpha + \cos^2 \alpha = 1 \qquad x^\circ =$$

$$\sqrt[n]{a^n} = a \qquad (\ln x)' = \frac{1}{x}$$

$$ax^2 + bx + c \qquad \int \frac{dx}{\sqrt{a+bx}}$$

$$(\sin x)' = \cos$$

What do a math test and Bray Wyatt have in common?

They both have a lot of problems.

What did one ring rope say to
the other ring rope?

"Meet you at the
CORNER!"

Why can't The
Phenomenal One
ever find clothes
that match?

The Styles Clash!

What kind of mus
makes Shawn
Michaels smile?

Sweet **GRIN**
Music.

What do you call a cow
that learns Strong Style?

Shinsuke Naka-**MOO**-ra!

Knock, knock.

Who's there?

Ittuzz.

Ittuzz wh—?

It doesn't matter who's there if you can **SMEEEEEL-L-L-L** what **THE ROCK** is cookin'!

What does Daniel Bryan say when he wants vegetable-peeling music?

Turnip the beets!

What do sick Kane and a volcano have in common?

They both spew fire!

Why did Ali eat his entrance gear?

He wanted a light snack.

Why are WWE Superstars bad at bowling?

Because they can only get one **PIN** at a time!

Which WWE Superstar is good at solving crimes?

R-Sleuth!

Why can't a WWE ref light a fire?

He always stops the **MATCH**.

What do The Hurricane, The Rock, and The Miz have in common?

They share a first name: "**THE**"!

What do Undertaker's bath towels say?

"His" and "Hearse."

Knock, knock.

Who's there?

Sheamus.

Sheamus who?

Sheamus not *WrestleMania* every day!

How does Charlotte Flair browse the internet?

On Charlotte's web!

What did Mr. T say when he was hired to be a principal?

"I pity the school!"

What do The Usos love to drink at lunch?

Uce boxes.

What do Road Dogg and Billy Gunn call their wives' parents?

The New Age In-Laws.

Why did the tailor bring his needles to the match?

So he could pin his opponent!

Knock, knock.

Who's there?

Ric Flair!

Ric Flair who?

No, Ric Flair . . .

. . . WOOOOOOO!

Why would elephants make great WWE Superstars?

They've already got the trunks!

Knock, knock.

Who's there?

Bayley.

Bayley who?

We Bayley made it home in time to watch *SmackDown Live!*

Why did the referee's feet smell when he was working?

Because he was on doodie!

What was **JAKE THE SNAKE**'s favorite subject in school?

Hisssss-tory!

47

Which WWE Legend is anxious all the time?

The Ultimate **WORRIER**!

What did Samoa Joe want after dinner?

SAMOA dessert!

Knock, knock.

Who's there?

Frosty.

Frosty who?

Frosty the **STROW**-man!

Which vegetable can fly the highest?

Sin Carrot!

Who did Undertaker
buy flowers for?

His ghoul-friend.

What does Zack Ryder say before serving dinner?

BRO-ne appétit!

What did Apollo Crews say when he accidentally ran into the old lady?

He Apollo-gized.

Why couldn't Curt Hawkins light his birthday candles?

He lost all his matches!

What does Buddy Murphy call a boomerang that doesn't come back?

A stick.

Which WWE Superstar never, ever flinches?

Ale-**STARE** Black!

What's the best room in Dwayne Johnson's house?

The kitchen. Because you can always smell what The Rock is cookin'!

Kiss the cook

Why can't Shawn Michaels be a cardiologist?

He's The Heartbreak Kid!

Which WWE Legend
grows in the forest?

Ba-tree-sta.

Which WWE event is the most respectful?

SIR-vivor Series.

What was Bret Hart's nickname in junior high?

"Zit Man."

What wears face paint and smells like a skunk?

Stink.

Which WWE Legend never gives up?

Mr. Practice-Makes-Perfect.

What's the best part of referee school?

Refe-recess.

Which WWE Superstar never shuts up?

Chat Gable (Also, Daniel Bryan).

Who is a pirate's favorite Superstar?

ARRRRR-Truth!

How can you tell if
UNDERTAKER
has a cold?

You can hear him coffin!

What's phenomenal
and makes you sneeze?

Hay-J Styles.

Did you hear the joke about the championship at stake in the ladder match?

It's over your head!

What does the **DESTROYER** rake up in the fall?

Bobby Lashleaves!

Which member of The New Day would take the best care of Francesca the trombone?

Xavier Would!

Who's the sneakiest
WWE Superstar?

The one you never
CENA coming!

Who did Bray Wyatt visit at the beach?

Sister **CRABIGAIL**.

Where is Jimmy Hart's chin?

South of the Mouth!

What does Roman Reigns drink at birthday parties?

Superman Punch!

CONGRATULATIONS!

You did it! Now, you're the funniest kid on the planet, capable of making your friends laugh so hard that milk shoots out of their noses like *WrestleMania* pyro! Go forth and harness your hilarity like the King or Queen of Crack-Ups that you are! (Just be sure to bring a towel for that milk pyro.)